I h

you already know how

much I appreciate your being the

dad to me that you didn't have to be.

But just in case you don't,

the words and sentiments in this book

express exactly how I feel

about you.

HE
DIDN'T
HAVE
~ TO BE

Brad Paisley and Kelley Lovelace

RUTLEDGE HILL PRESS® • *Nashville, Tennessee*

Published by Rutledge Hill Press, a division of Thomas Nelson, Inc., P.O. Box 141000, Nashville, Tennessee 37214.
www.ThomasNelson.com

Photos on pages front endsheet, 10, 16, 22–23, 28–29, 30, 39, 46–47, 49, 50–51, 52, and 64 licensed through Photodisc.
Photos on pages 15, 19, 25, and 44 licensed through StockMarket.
Photo on page 43 licensed through Eyewire Photo.
Photo on page 4 by Nigel Parry and used by permission.
Photo on pages 60–61 by Chris Hollo used by permission.
Photo opposite title page courtesy of Jennifer Greenstein;
photo on page 13 courtesy of Danny Ragland; photo on page 33 courtesy of Vance Lawson;
photo on page 34 by Susan Cooper and courtesy of Bob Cooper;
photo on pages 37 and 62 by Karen Lovelace and courtesy of Kelley Lovelace;
photo on page 55 by Reneé Skaggs Crowell; photo on back endsheet by Leah Gilliam.
All photos used by permission.

Design by Gore Studio, Inc., Nashville, Tennessee

ISBN: 1-55853-935-2

Printed in the United States of America

01 02 03 04 05 — 5 4 3 2 1

WE DEDICATE THIS BOOK

to our families,

and

we give thanks to God

for allowing us to write a song

that has helped us and others gratefully express

feelings of love and appreciation to fathers for

being the dads they didn't have to be.

—BRAD PAISLEY
—KELLEY LOVELACE

My album was finished, or so we thought. Due to scheduling difficulties and market congestion, Arista Records waited until February 1999 to release the album and single, "Who Needs Pictures." This left a lot of time to kill. While in that holding pattern, I was able to spend a great deal of time with friend and cowriter Kelley Lovelace and his new family. You see, Kelley married Karen, who had a child from a previous marriage. At the time of the marriage, her child, McCain Merren, was six years old. He is now ten. Anyway, Kelley and I decided to write one night after dinner. Once Karen and McCain had gone to bed, we sat on their back porch and wrote about the relationship that had developed between McCain and Kelley.

The neat thing about this song is that it was not written in the typical Music Row fashion. There was no appointment and no office. There were just two friends sitting on a porch while the subjects we were writing about were asleep inside. I remember finishing it quickly compared to most songs that we write. I looked at Kelley and said, "Ya know, I'm not sure either one of us is a good enough writer to have just written this song." Kelley replied, "I'm not either, but I don't see anyone else on this porch so I think we should put our names on it." I think we both realized that we had something special.

Looking back over countless letters, e-mails, stories, and testimonies from listeners all across the country, I am convinced that this song was divinely inspired. I think this will always be my favorite song I've ever written.

I learned a valuable lesson from this song. By writing something that meant so much personally, with no commercial aspirations, we wound up achieving the formula for songs with an impact: honesty and reality.

—BRAD PAISLEY

HE DIDN'T HAVE TO BE

❖ ❖ ❖

When a single mom goes out on a date with somebody new,
It always winds up feeling more like a job interview.
My momma used to wonder if she'd ever meet someone
Who wouldn't find out about me and then turn around and run.

I met the man I call my dad when I was five years old.
He took my mom out to a movie and for once I got to go.
A few months later I remember lying there in bed.
I overheard him pop the question and I prayed that she'd say yes.

And then all of a sudden it seemed so strange to me
How we went from "something's missing" to a family.
Looking back, all I can say about all the things he did for me
Is I hope I'm at least half the dad
That he didn't have to be.

I met the girl that's now my wife about three years ago.
We had the perfect marriage but we wanted something more.
Now here I stand surrounded by our family and friends,
Crowded 'round the nursery window as they bring the baby in.

And now all of a sudden it seems so strange to me
How we've gone from "something's missing" to a family.
Looking through the glass, I think about the man that's standing next to me
And I hope I'm at least half the dad
That he didn't have to be.

Looking back, all I can say about all the things he did for me
Is I hope I'm at least half the dad
That he didn't have to be.
Yeah, I hope I'm at least half the dad
That he didn't have to be
Because he didn't have to be,
You know he didn't have to be.

LET'S TAKE IT FROM THE TOP...

7

WHEN A single mom goes out on a date with somebody new,

It always
winds up feeling
more like a
job interview.

A nervous single mom speeds off to meet *yet another first date* for dinner after work one night. She arrives a little late, but the way he smiles when he sees her lets her know he doesn't mind. He tells her that she looks incredible and that he has looked forward to this night all week long. After they both order what is sure to be a fabulous meal, he leans across the table with his undivided attention and says, "So tell me all about yourself."

For the fourth time this year, she tells herself this could be the one. So with complete confidence she begins safely by telling him where she works and what she does while she's there. She briefly complains about her boss and follows with, "But overall, he's a really nice man." She mentions how well she gets along with most all of her coworkers and then smoothly makes the transition into talking about where she grew up, her mom, and her dad. Then as the butterflies get restless and take flight in her stomach, her mouth utters the mother of all date-ending phrases:

"BUT THE MOST IMPORTANT THING IN MY LIFE IS MY LITTLE ALEX."

Hoping that "My Little Alex" is a goldfish, cat, or maybe even one of those cute little Maltese dogs, her date says, "and Alex is ...?"

"My five-year-old boy," she says. "Would you like to see his picture?"

Trying his best to maintain a smile, he nauseously says, "Oh, you have one with you?"

After he has viewed the picture for the required amount of time for getting credit for a sincere look, he says, "Ah, he's a cute little fella."

The truth is, it wouldn't matter if the picture displayed an actual angelic halo hovering above the divine little creature. In most cases, the date is just a few bites away from being over.

❖ ❖ ❖

As great as Mom is,
anyone could have loved her.
But she knew it would take
someone really special
to love me too.

I'm so glad Mom

DIDN'T

give up before

she found

you!

15

My momma

used to wonder if she'd
ever meet someone
Who wouldn't find out
about me and then turn
around and run.

She
wasn't
the
only one
who
wondered
that.

THE FIRST TIME
you came to the door
To pick up our Mom for a date,
We knew you were
the one!

HOW DOES IT FEEL TO HAVE SUCH SMART KIDS?

Sometimes it takes

years

for someone to
save the

day.

Until my stepdad came into my life there was no such thing as a "Happy Birthday" or a "Merry Christmas." I remember pouting around the house saying things like, "What's there to be happy about and what's so merry about Christmas?" I was just a kid back then, and what I wanted more than anything was to have a dad.

You know, Mom, it's funny. He's been in our lives for so long now that I can hardly remember a time when he wasn't there. I thank God that I had him while I was growing up and that you still have him now that I'm grown.

I love you both.

—*Anonymous*, Tennessee

But when that special someone arrives,

the long wait is quickly forgotten.

I MET THE MAN
I call my dad
When I was five years old.
He took my mom
out to a movie
And for once I got to go.

I met my husband when my son was eight years old. He suggested that we take my son with us on our first date. My son is now twenty-eight years old. He's getting married, and he still has the world's best dad.

Sometimes at a wedding the son dedicates a song to his mother. Although he will do that, he's also going to dedicate your song to his dad.

—*Donna*, FLORIDA

A FEW MONTHS

later I remember
Lying there in bed.
I overheard him
pop the question
And I prayed that she'd
say yes. *Oh Mom, please say yes.*

If I had a dad
Oh what I could see,
On top of his shoulders
Way up in the trees.

If I had a dad
Oh what I could hear:
"You can do it," "I'm proud of you,"
and "We'll get 'em next year."

If I had a dad
Oh what I could be,
With his loving presence
To encourage me.

If I had a dad
Oh what I could do—
Anything and everything
I set my mind to.

I have a stepdad who has done so much for me in my life and I love him deeply. I wish he could have been my dad from the day I was born.

—*Cory,* FLORIDA
(nine years old)

31

The word

"Mom"

just doesn't sound
or feel complete
until it's
followed by

"and Dad."

You complete

US.

Are
dads
REALLY
that
important?

A cover article in *U.S. News & World Report*
concluded that …

DAD IS DESTINY.

❖ ❖ ❖

It said that more than any other factor,
a father's presence in the family will
determine a child's success and happiness.

I am who I am because of my stepdad. There's one story in particular that turned my life around.

My stepdad had been in my life since I was two. However, I had come to a point when I took him and everything else for granted. I was in the ninth grade and I was cutting class with some of my friends to take a drive and a smoke. It was a bitter cold winter day and as we were driving, we passed this guy walking on the side of the road. One of my friends said, "Oh man, I'd hate to be that guy. It's too cold out there to walk." As we drove past the man, I looked out the back window and saw that it was my stepdad. That was the four-mile stretch of road that he walked every day from the local college straight to work so that he could support me.

From that day on, I took my life seriously. I finished high school and then went to LSU and graduated with a degree in architecture. This man was a huge influence on my life, and I love him with all my heart.

—*Chris*, Louisiana

Children

crave

the love of a father.

Not just someone who
is physically there,
but someone who is
there whole-
heartedly
(physically,
emotionally,
and
spiritually).

Though my real dad left my mom and me before I knew him, I feel as though I have been blessed because I know that I have the best stepdad of all time.

He didn't just love my mom. He truly loved me. I know this because he spent so much of his time alone with just me. He taught me everything I know how to do today.

One of my fondest memories is the first time he took me fishing. I was about seven years old. I had no idea what I was doing, but he comforted me by saying, "they're really tough to catch today, little buddy." A couple of hours passed, and my stepdad finally got a fish on his line. After seeing my excitement, he waved me over so I could help him reel it in. He said that it was the biggest crappie he had ever seen and that he couldn't have caught it without me.

To this day Mom still thinks I caught that fish.

—*Danny*, GEORGIA

Is there
anything
a single mom
can't do
for her
children?

In this day and time we would be crazy to give an affirmative answer to this question. However, God created us in such a way that there are

CERTAIN THINGS

that dads tend to handle better than moms.

The opposite, of course, also holds true, but that's a whole different song and book.

❖ ❖ ❖

A few of these *dad things* are…

Teaching
a
little boy
how
to
bait a hook.

*(Without saying
yuk or ewww).*

43

Being a full-time punching bag and being ready to wrestle at any given moment (making them think you're invincible no matter how hard they hit or kick—even if it's killing you).

Attending father/son and father/daughter picnics.

Or someday having the opportunity to be the best man at her son's wedding or giving away the bride when her daughter ties the knot.

A single mom also won't be able to demonstrate to her son how a loving husband is supposed to treat his wife.

Or be able to give her daughter a daily example of how a wife loves her husband.

THE
GREATEST
THING

a father can do
for his children is to
love their mother.

—Josh McDowell

I Love You, Karen.

—Kelley

I never thought of my stepfather as a "stepfather" because, I suppose, he never really tried to take the place of my dad.

Now that I'm grown and married myself, I've come to understand the kind of man it takes to have married into a broken family with three adolescents.

He has always been a great friend, and even helped me paint my car—twice! But even more important, he has taught me by example that a man in marriage and in life can have dignity, grace, patience, and love. God knows my life would never have been the same without him.

— *Tim*, Tennessee

So when the biological father is not in the picture for whatever reason and a loving stepfather steps up to the plate with the bases loaded and a full count and proceeds to hit the ball out of the park on a daily basis for the rest of his life... what does that make him?

HERO

has a nice ring to it!

(Kelley wrote that)
—Brad

50

He-ro 2. A person noted for feats of courage or nobility of purpose, especially one who has risked or sacrificed his life.

(*The American Heritage Dictionary*, Houghton Mifflin Company)

Thanks for taking

RISKS

and making

SACRIFICES!

As I was thinking today, I realized how much you do for me! If it's not coaching my baseball team, it's roller-blading with me. I cannot stress enough how much I love you.

The day you and Mom got married was one of the best days of my life. You didn't have to be my dad, but I'm sure glad you are.

— *Jameson*, GEORGIA
(ten years old)

AND THEN
all of a sudden
It seemed so strange to me
How we went from
"something's missing"
to a family.

Dear Mr. Paisley,

One of the few pleasures I enjoy in prison is the occasional opportunity to watch country music videos. I must say I was mesmerized by your new song, "He Didn't Have to Be." I watched the video unashamed of the tears rolling down my face. After you've read my story, you'll understand why your performance affected me so.

Charles P. was the husband of my cousin Karen. Not many people would willingly step into a tragedy, but that is exactly what Charles and Karen chose to do when they volunteered to raise my two little girls. Mandy was five and Lyndsey was three when I was sent to prison fifteen years ago.

And thus began Charles's transformation into the dad he didn't have to be. The whole mess involved his wife's family. Yet, he <u>chose</u> to be the one who bandaged skinned knees and wiped runny noses. He was there when the kids lost their first tooth and rode their first bike. He drove them to ball practice and was a willing guinea pig for their first cooking efforts. He shared their laughter and dried their tears.

When you ask the kids about their memories of growing up in his house, you're apt to hear stories of good-humored pranks and laughter—like the time he told a daughter to howl like mad as he gave her a well deserved paddling. Only later did we learn he was belting the couch for sound effects instead. He was the one they ran to when a hug or helping hand was needed. He was quick to laugh, slow to anger, and kind to all.

Charles P. died in August 1998 after a long battle with leukemia. He died too soon. The good ones always do, it seems. He died too soon to walk our daughters down the aisle. He died too soon for me to ever have the chance to adequately thank him for being the dad he didn't have to be.

There must have been times in your career when you wondered if all your work was worth it. Let me tell you, friend, if you never win a Grammy, you've already done more good than you will ever know.

—*Charles S.*, TEXAS

LOOKING BACK,
all I can say
About all the things
he did for me
Is I hope I'm at least
half the dad
That he didn't have to be.

Being a guy I hate to admit this, but I sat down and cried the other day when I heard your song. You see, Jacob, our first child, was born a few weeks ago and my stepfather (the man I really do call "Dad") was there at the hospital with my wife and me. Without a doubt, the proudest moment in my life was placing our son in my dad's arms for the first time. I can only hope that Jacob grows up to love and respect me as much as I do my dad.

—Mark, MASSACHUSETTS

59

Early in my career, I was playing at a rodeo in the Midwest. I woke up late to find a police officer standing outside the bus, and my road manager said he'd been there all morning. I ventured outside wondering who in the world had requested that kind of security for a new and virtually unknown artist like me.

I was greeted with a firm handshake from a man who was visibly emotional about getting to tell me his story. He said he'd taken a half day off from work, hoping that he would somehow manage to thank me personally for my song about "the stepdad."

"Two weeks ago," he began, " I lost my best friend. My Da …" And then came the tears. After pulling himself together, he explained that his dad (his stepdad actually, but only by title), had been in a fatal car wreck. However, just a few weeks earlier the officer had heard my song and found the courage to tell his dad how much he loved him. He was quite sure he never would have done that if he had not heard the song. He had waited all morning just to thank me for something I had no idea I had done.

I thought back to the night we wrote the song, to the effortless way it seemed to just appear on the page, and the feeling I'd had about God somehow gifting us with a song He wanted to exist; and I could totally see a much bigger plan.

This was one of the first testimonials I had heard of what this song meant to someone else, and thousands were to follow. Every one of them has reaffirmed my belief that someone much bigger than Kelley or myself actually penned it. "Writer," this time, means we wrote it down. That's all.

—BRAD PAISLEY

Dear McCain,

Once again, you and your mom are sound asleep, but Brad and I aren't writing a song this time. He went home a little while ago after we wrote the last page of this book and agreed that it was finally done. As I was getting ready for bed, the thought occurred to me that I was missing an opportunity to tell you how I feel about you. So I decided to sneak this page in so you'll know how important you are to me. I'll tell Brad about it later. *After it's gone to press.*

Before I married your mom, I struggled with the thought of becoming an instant father. I mean, from what I had heard about how difficult things can be the first few years of marriage, I wondered how much more difficult it might be starting out with a six-year-old.

I asked myself a lot of questions. Could I handle sharing my wife with someone else? Could I possibly love you as if you were my own? Would I still remember how to do math problems when you needed help with your homework? In short, could I handle the incredible responsibilities of being a dad?

Well, with the exception of having to re-learn fractions, the answers to the other questions are all yes. However, I can't take the credit. How could I not love you? Everyone tells me what a great guy I am for doing what I've done. It's funny, I wish they knew how great you are. You make my job easy.

You make my smile bigger
My laugh harder
My life fuller
And my heart stronger.

I want to thank you in advance for all the joy you'll bring to my life in the future. I love you!

—KELLEY

MY ONLY REGRET IN MY LIFE IS

THAT IT WAS ALWAYS SO DIFFICULT

TO LET MY FATHER KNOW THE GREAT

DEPTH OF MY AFFECTION

FOR HIM.

—*Dwight D. Eisenhower*

64

God gave me life.

Jesus gave me hope.

You gave me love.

❖ ❖ ❖

Thanks,

"DAD"